The Royal Spanish Military Hospital of Saint Augustine

By

Dr. Christine Miller

The Royal Spanish Military Hospital of Saint Augustine
By Christine Miller
Cover design by Vincent Rospond
This edition published in 2019

Published in conjunction with Winged Hussar Publishing, an imprint of
Pike and Powder Publishing Group LLC
1525 Hulse Rd, Unit 1   1 Craven Lane, Box 66066
Point Pleasant, NJ 08742   Lawrence, NJ 08648-66066
https://wingedhussarpublishing.com

Copyright © Christine Miller
ISBN 978-1-
LCN

Bibliographical References and Index
1. History. 2. US Colonial. 3. Florida

Visit The Royal Spanish Military Hospital of Saint Augustine at:
http://www.spanishmilitaryhospitalmuseum.com

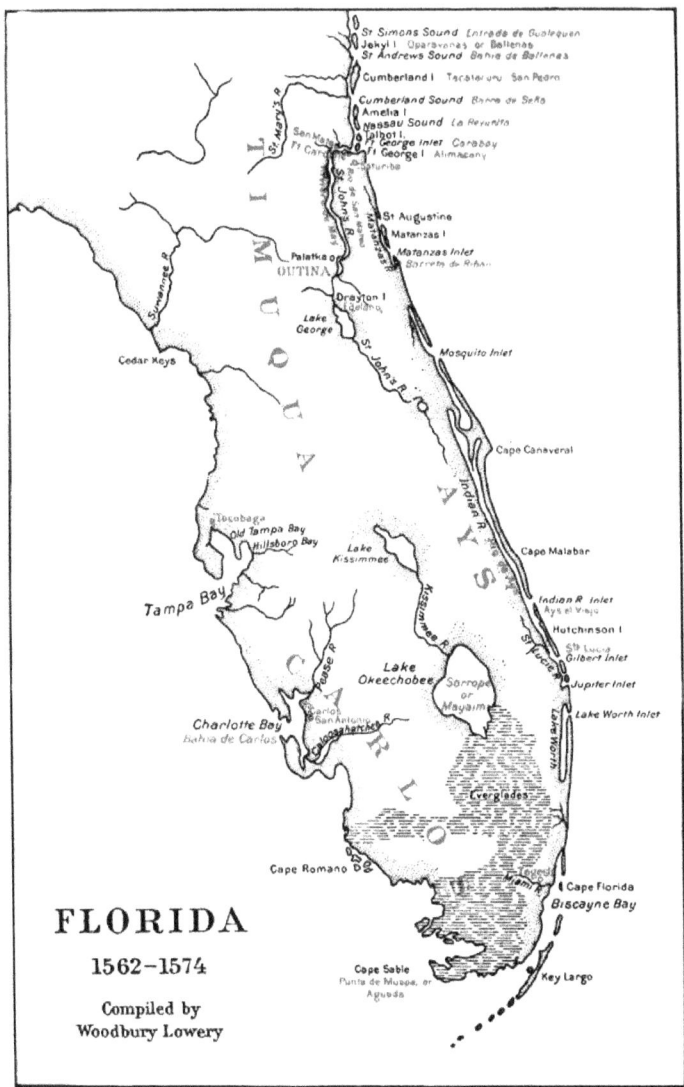

St Simons Sound Entrada de Gualequen
Jekyl I Oparvanas or Ballenas
St Andrews Sound Bahia de Ballenas

Cumberland I Tacatacuru San Pedro

Cumberland Sound Barra de Seña
Amelia I
Nassau Sound La Reunita
Talbot I.
George Inlet Caraboy
Ft George I Alimacany

St Mary's R.
San Mateo
Ft Caroline
Saturiba

Saturiba

R. de San Mateo

St Johns R.

St Augustine

Matanzas I

Matanzas Inlet
Barretos de Ribau

Palatka or
OUTINA

R. San Mateo

Drayton I
Edelano

Lake
George

St Johns R.

Mosquito Inlet

Suwannee R.

Cedar Keys

Cape Canaveral

M   U   Q   U   A   Y   S

Indian R. Ays

Tocobaga
Old Tampa Bay
Hillsboro Bay

Lake
Kissimmee

Cape Malabar

Tampa Bay

Indian R. Inlet
Ays el Viejo

Hutchinson I

Kissimmee R.

St Lucia
Gilbert Inlet

Lake
Okeechobee

Sarrope
or
Mayaimi

Jupiter Inlet

Lake Worth Inlet

St Lucie

Lake Worth

Charlotte Bay
Bahia de Carlos

Carlos
San Antonio
Caloosahatchee R.

Everglades

C   A   L   O   S

F   L   O

Cape Romano

Cape Florida
Biscayne Bay

FLORIDA

1562–1574

Compiled by
Woodbury Lowery

Cape Sable
Punta de Muspa, or
Aguada

Key Largo

Spanish Florida

The city of Saint Augustine (San Augustin) was founded in 1565 by Pedro Menendez de Aviles thus beginning the 1st Spanish period in La Florida. This town was the center of the mission system where the Franciscan Order with the backing of the Spanish crown began to convert the indigenous population to Catholicism. The converted native population were required to perform hard physical labor to support the Spanish colony. The 1st Spanish Period ended in 1763, when the British won the Seven Years War and Spain was forced to relinquish Florida to retain Cuba, a far more profitable holding.

Figure 1- St. Augustine Founder-Pedro Menendez (history.org)

Viva Espana!

Spain returns to Florida in 1784 (2nd Spanish Period) after the British defeat in the American Revolution! The new Governor, Vincente Manuel de Zespedes and his chief engineer Mariano de la Roque, found many buildings left from the British Period to be dilapidated and uninhabitable. Restoring St. Augustine would be a daunting task indeed!

Fun Fact: Spain provided financial and naval support to the American cause during the Revolutionary War

The need to establish a proper military hospital to care for soldiers and sailors stationed at the garrison (Castillo de San Marcos) was a priority. The provisional hospital location chosen was on the lot that formerly belonged to William Watson, a Scottish carpenter, who fled with other British subjects once Spain regained control of the region. The stable portion of the Watson property was used as a medical center (east complex) starting in 1791. The residential portion served as living quarters for the chief apothecary, Ramon de Fuentes. The Royal Military Hospital was named in honor of the coronation of King Charles IV of Spain as well as to the glory of Our Lady of Guadalupe.

Figure 2-Our Lady of Guadalupe, Feast Day December 12th (catholic.org)

The west complex was located nearby (on the corner of modern-day King Street and A1A) but little historic information has been uncovered regarding this site other than some notation that this complex burns down in 1818.

*Fun Fact: Governor Zespedes held a 3-day long celebration in 1789 to celebrate the new reign of King Charles IV! Many colonial towns celebrated this way to gain the monarch's favor. Que Fiesta!!!

Figure 3- King Charles IV of Spain (biography.com)

Hospital Protocol

The Spanish Empire since the reign of Ferdinand and Isabella placed great importance on the public health within Spain and all of its territories by ensuring high standards in medical care. The Royal Protomedicato was board of physicians appointed by the Spanish Crown to regulate all medical professions. This governing body set standards for education requirements, licensing, and regular on-site inspection for all medical disciplines. The Spanish military also held strict standards for the various healthcare professionals who served in its royal hospitals around the world.

Fun Fact: Spain's medical practices were greatly influenced by Islamic principles of quarantine for the sickest patients and ritual cleansing during patient care resulting in better outcomes. The Moors controlled most of the Iberian Peninsula prior to the 15th century

Daily Operations

Figure 4- Hospital Bells from The Spanish Military Hospital Museum

Rounding on all patients in the hospital twice a day was mandatory, the times set were as follows: during the summer months 5am and in the afternoon at 3pm, in winter months 6am and in the afternoon at 2pm. The bells located in the front of the hospital were rung three times to signal the beginning of hospital rounds. The physician, pharmacist, ward attendant and medical interns all participated in hospital rounds.

*Fun Fact: medical interns were not allowed to cut the hair of any patients in the hospital unless there was an order from the physician. This policy was a sanitary measure as lice infestations were common in the 18th century

Hospital Menu

Figure 5 - Salted pork was staple food in military rations in the 18th century(savoringthepast.net)

Ordinary rations for each day were set as one pound of fresh beef, one ounce of bacon, beans, and half of an ounce of pork lard. This would be distributed in the following manner:

Breakfast
Soup made from 2 ounces of break and half an ounce of lard

Mid-day
8 ounces of beef, half an ounce of beans, half an ounce of bacon, and 6 ounces of bread

Supper

An equal quantity set aside from the mid-day meal

Mourning Room

Figure 6-Mourning Room at the Spanish Military Hospital Museum

The mourning room held the bodies of soldiers to be laid out for a 24-hour period prior to burial. The hospital chaplain, Father Francisco Traconis, would perform the sacrament of anointing the sick (last rites) and provided spiritual comfort to the family of the deceased. The chaplain was also responsible for hearing the confessions of all patients upon admission to the hospital.

Doctor's Office

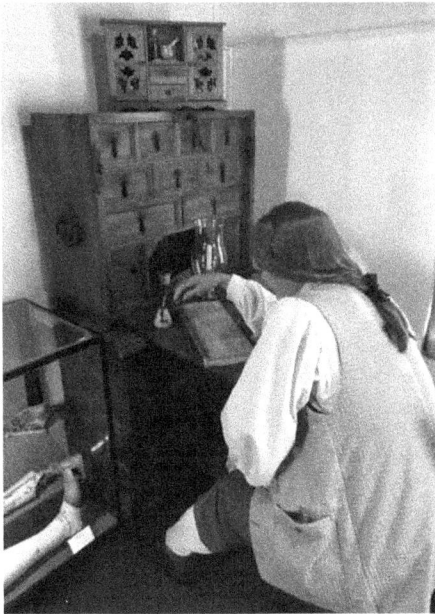

Figure 7- Hospital Physician-Dr. Tomas Travers

The lead physician in the early years of the Spanish Military Hospital was Dr. Tomas Travers. He was a Roman Catholic from Ireland that came to Saint Augustine initially with the British army. When Spain regained control, Dr. Travers stayed and became a Spanish citizen. The head surgeon of the hospital was Juan Jose Bousquet. The Administrator, Juan Manuel Sezantes, was

responsible for all financial activity including fin-
ing patients who did not follow hospital policy.
Nursing roles were performed by older soldiers
who assisted in the daily care of their comrades
in arms.

*Fun Fact: In 1786 a royal order allowed all
previous British residents to stay in Saint
Augustine if they swore allegiance to Spain
and became Roman Catholic.*

The Ward Rooms

Figure 8-Officers Ward, Spanish Military Hospital Museum

    The Royal Military Hospital had 3 ward rooms, the officers' ward which contained wooden bed frames and mattresses, the enlisted men's' ward that only had mattresses on the floor, and lastly the isolation ward, for the sickest patients to be separated from the general patient population. Hospital policy mandated that the wards could not be too crowded and that sanitary standards be maintained at all times. The ward attendant was charged with ensuring linens and clothing from the isolation ward were washed separately to prevent disease transmission. Removing bed bugs and other insects from all hospital mattresses along with setting up rat traps were part of his duties. The ward attendants had living quarters on the 2nd floor of the hospital.

Apothecary Shop

Figure 9- The Apothecary Shop, Spanish Military Hospital

The chief apothecary, Ramon de Fuentes, had the responsibility of preparing all the medications in a timely fashion that were ordered by the physician. His knowledge of herbal medicine was extensive. His position required participation in hospital rounds daily. Ramon de Fuentes lived next door to the hospital, in the former Watson residence, and tended the garden that stretched in between the two structures. Importing medicine from other parts of the Spanish empire was expensive and funding was always scarce in Saint Augustine.

Figure 10- Hospital Garden (the Watson house is in the background) at the Spanish Military Hospital

Spanish apothecaries needed to learn about herbal remedies from local plants, so they relied upon the knowledge of the native people of La Florida. The Timucua inhabited most of modern-day north Florida and southern Georgia. These indigenous people had continuous contact with the Spanish since 1565 and were paramount to colonial survival.

Figure 11- Timucuan Chief performing Black Drink Ceremony (wikipedia.org)

Fun Fact: The leaves of the yaupon holly were dried and used as a tea by the Timucua called "The Black Drink" that was consumed by warriors prior to battle. Yaupon holly leaves contain a large amount of caffeine. The Spanish used this tea both medicinally and recreationally calling it cassina.

Figure 12- Yaupon holly (IIex vomitoria)-wikipedia.org

The American Territorial Era

The Royal Military Hospital functioned steadily throughout the 2nd Spanish period. Starting in early 1821, Saint Augustine began transitioning from Spanish rule to becoming an American territory. During the summer of 1821, the city experienced a horrific yellow fever outbreak. The military hospital was then utilized for the general population during the darkest days of the yellow fever epidemic. Unfortunately, many records from this period did not survive. In 1895, a fire burns down the hospital east complex.

The Modern Era

In the late 1960s through the early 1970s, there was a renewed historic interest in Saint Augustine's colonial past! The Florida Medical Association in partnership with the Saint Augustine Historical Restoration & Preservation Committee utilized archeologic records to reconstruct the Spanish Military Hospital into the Florida Medical History Museum. This museum left the 1st floor as it was during the 2nd Spanish period and included medical exhibits on the 2nd floor that previously served as the hospital attendants' quarters. By the 1980's the Florida Medical History Museum plagued with financial issues had closed.

Today, the Spanish Military Hospital Museum features the ground floor, as it would have been during the years of hospital operation. The current owners have done meticulous research to ensure historic accuracy regarding the medical treatment and overall patient care appropriate to this time frame. The second floor is not currently used for exhibits, but future plans do include usage of that space to enhance this gem located on Aviles Street in the heart of the historic district. The lush garden is filled with medicinal herbs such as valerian root, aloe, calendula, mint, and camphor that are used for demonstrations during the apothecary portion by museum tour guides

Fun Fact: The Spanish Military Hospital Museum is one of the few historic sites in Saint Augustine that reflect the 2nd Spanish Period (1784-1821)

Figure 13-Soldiers being treated at the Royal Military Hospital by Future Historian, Vincent Piraino-age 6

Bibliography

Bakhtiar, Laleh, comp. Avicenna On The Four Humours, Sanguinous/Serous/Bilious/Atrabilious. Trans. O. Carmen Gunner. New York: Great of the Islamic World, 1999. Print.

"Brochure for Military Hospital." University of Florida Digital Collections.: n.p., n.d. N. page. Smathers Library. Web. 15 July 2015. <http:/ufdc.ufl.edu//UF00094843/00001>.

"Historical Research Notes on Block 28, Lot 2 and Military Hospital." St. Augustine Historical Association and Preservation Commission. 1-25. University of Florida Digital Records. Web. 10 July 2015. <http://ufdc.ufl.edu/UF00094843/00002>.

Hoffman, Paul E. "New Tidewater Frontiers, 1763-1790." Florida's Frontiers. Bloomington: Indiana UP, 2002. 236-37. Print.

Johnson, Sherry. "The Spanish St. Augustine Community, 1784

Lanning, John Tate., and John Jay. TePaske. The Royal Protomedicato: The Regulation of the Medical Professions in the Spanish Empire. Durham,

NC: Duke UP, 1985. Print.

Milanich, Jerald T. Laboring in the Fields of the Lord: Spanish Missions and Southeastern Indians. Univ. Press of Florida, 2006.

Rashid, Harunor, and Shafquat Mohammed Rafiq. "Islamic Prevention of Avian Influenza." J Islam Med Assoc Journal of the Islamic Medical Association of North America 39.3 (2007): 121-26. Web. 10 July 2015

"Regulations for Interior Political and Economic Government of Hospitals in the Island of Cuba." University of Florida Digital Collections. n.d. 1-3. Web. <http://ufdc.ufl.edu//UF00094840/00008>.

"St. Augustine Hospital." University of Florida Digital Collections. n.p., 1975. N. page. Web. <http://ufdc.ufl.edu//UF00094840/00009>.

"Spanish Military Hospital." Historic St. Augustine Preservation Board, Division of Cultural Affairs. n.d. 1-4. University of Florida Digital Collections. Web. 10 July 2015. <http://ufdc.ufl.edu// USAC00001/00004>.

Tanner, Helen Hornbeck. "The 1789 Saint Augustine Celebration." The Florida Historical Quarterly, vol. 38, no. 4, 1 Apr. 1960, pp. 280–293.

Find out more about the Spanish Military hospital at:

www.spanishmilitaryhospitalmuseum.com

www.ingramcontent.com/pod-product-compliance
Lightning Source LLC
Chambersburg PA
CBHW051233020426
42331CB00016B/3360